The text printed here is taken from *Collected Poems* (1950). I have arranged the poems according to their appearance in individual volumes. No selection has been made from Yeats's longer narrative and dramatic poems.

G. D.

GU00372866

CONTENTS

INTRODUCTION

In January 1939, W.B. Yeats died and was buried in France. After the hostilities of the Second World War had ceased, he was finally laid to rest in 1948 in a little Protestant churchyard at Drumcliff, County Sligo. His work as a poet was traded in for his name and we were bequeathed a phenomenon: *Yeatsian.*

Two things happened in the fifty-odd years that separate us from Yeats's death. For many in Ireland and elsewhere, knowledge of his poetry shrank to a few hardy annuals that recurred in anthologies kept at home or the teaching texts at school. 'The Fiddler of Dooney', 'The Lake Isle of Innisfree' and some of the more 'difficult' poems such as 'Leda and the Swan' and 'Byzantium'. Simultaneously, Yeats became an industry, with an entire academic mill churning out critical volumes on his life, poetry, drama, prose writing, reading and mythologies.

Between the two worlds — of either scant familiarity or the monumental expert consumption of Yeats and what he stood for as an individual public figure — we lost sight of Yeats the poet.

Critics and scholars will argue until the cows come home about who and what the essential Yeats *is* precisely. Many see him as an old right-wing fogey who is tainted for life by his brief flirtation with Irish national socialism; others mock him as a relic of Auld Dacency, his head in the clouds, best left to tourist promoters of an Ireland no longer (if ever) *real*. But can there actually be a central core to any writer's work, we might like to ask? After all, times change and our ways of seeing things alter and in so doing radically affect what we look at, as much as how we do the looking.

One fact however is indisputable: the international standing of Irish poetry is due to William Butler Yeats. His achievement, principally as a poet but also as a critic, dramatist and polemicist for Irish cultural nationalism, is the pivotal point around which the direction of Irish poetry is most often drawn. Yet there is a contradiction here. For, in spite of the tremendous influence Yeats exerted throughout his own lifetime — in Ireland and Europe, the United States and across language barriers world-wide — his poetic legacy within Ireland has taken a back seat to the cultural and political significance of his life and times. This is the context in which his poetry is fiercely debated by critics. Yet the artistic inheritance, by comparison, remains somewhat *unacknowledged* by poets of today.

During his long life, however, W.B. Yeats transformed Irish poetry (in the English language) from its uncertain beginnings in the nineteenth century — the sprawling mythological epics of Sir Samuel Ferguson (1810-86), the martial ballads of Thomas Davis (1814-45), James Clarence Mangan's (1803-49) exotic and introverted autobiographical masques — into a language of what he was to call 'passionate syntax'. In 'To Ireland in the Coming Times' (*The Rose*, 1893) Yeats proclaims his allegiance to the company of Davis, Mangan and Ferguson as poets who

> *...sang, to sweeten Ireland's wrong,*
> *Ballad and story, rann and song;*
> *Nor be I any less of them,*
> *Because of the red-rose-bordered hem*
> *Of her, whose history began*
> *Before God made the angelic clan,*
> *Trails all about the written page.*

During the turbulent years ahead, Yeats continuously redefined this allegiance, as Ireland lurched first into class struggle (the 1913 lockout), rebellion and executions (Easter 1916), then into the War of Independence (1919-21) and finally the Civil War (1922-23) before the state was actually founded, albeit within a partitioned country.

'September 1913', for instance, opens with a powerful sense of disillusionment that the high, lofty ideals of nationalists such as Yeats's friend and mentor, John O'Leary, had ignominiously dwindled into conniving religiosity and commercial self-interest:

> What need you, being come to sense,
> But fumble in a greasy till
> And add the halfpence to the pence
> And prayer to shivering prayer, until
> You have dried the marrow from the bone?
> For men were born to pray and save:
> Romantic Ireland's dead and gone,
> It's with O'Leary in the grave.

Most critics agree that *Responsibilities* (1914), the collection from which this poem comes, marks a substantial change in Yeats's poetry with diction and rhythm much more clearly defined. Probably under the influence of his friend Ezra Pound, who was acting as a secretary to him at this time (1913-14), Yeats broke from the customary crepuscular ambiguities which had characterised the earlier poetry, and created in collections such as *Responsibilities* and *The Wild Swans at Coole* (1919), a stark imagistic simplicity unburdened with literary conceit:

> The trees are in their autumn beauty,
> The woodland paths are dry,
> Under the October twilight the water
> Mirrors a still sky;
> Upon the brimming water among the stones
> Are nine, and, fifty swans.

The remaining twenty years of his life were to prove remarkably creative for Yeats the poet. He pursued his own intuitive needs into the supernatural, an obsession since he was a young man, and simultaneously proposed a view of civilisation and history that, while veering towards the fascist movements current in the late 1920s and '30s, insisted upon the essential integrity and significance of the poetic imagination to the modern world.

In poems such as 'The Fisherman' and 'Ego Dominus Tuus' (*The Wild Swans at Coole*) Yeats explored his ambition, as he says in the former poem, to write 'one/Poem maybe as cold/And passionate as the dawn', conscious, all the while, as he stated in the latter poem, that

> ...art
> Is but a vision of reality.
> What portion in the world can the artist have
> Who has awakened from the common dream
> But dissipation and despair?

It is the rhetorical question which Yeats's poetry constantly sought to answer, sometimes in an over-elaborate symbolic construction, like 'The Phases of the Moon' (*The Wild Swans at Coole*), but also in the naturalistic style of 'Easter 1916' or 'Sixteen Dead Men', where contemporary life is turned into art.

Never far from Yeats's mind, though, was his particular sense of himself as a poet and the need to *create* a suitable landscape and vision of life which could house his imagination. In 'Sailing to Byzantium' (*The Tower*, 1928) Yeats wishes to dwell, figuratively, in 'the artifice of eternity', cele-brating, with an almost Keatsian sensuousness, the glorious Byzantine world, 'to sing.../Of what is past, or passing, or to come'. This desire always gives way in Yeats's poetry to a rigorous refusal to give up on the world and, while there are many poems in which he curses the modern world and what he sees as its graceless and glum unheroic failings, Yeats returns to that 'real' world, often with a vengeance, as in 'Blood and the Moon':

There, on blood-saturated ground, have stood
Soldier, assassin, executioner,
Whether for daily pittance or in blind fear,
Or out of abstract hatred, and shed blood...

In sequences such as 'The Tower', 'Meditations in Time of Civil War', 'Nineteen Hundred and Nineteen' — all published in *The Tower* — and 'Blood and the Moon' (*The Winding Stair and Other Poems,* 1933) from which the above quotation is taken, Yeats set down powerfully forthright terms of reference for those poets who were publishing or beginning their writing careers in the mid-to-late 1930s. This ensured that in his *Last Poems* (1936-39), Yeats spoke with an indisputable authority not only on the recent history of his country, a history that he and friends like Lady Gregory had in part shaped, but, more crucially, of the place that he had confirmed for poetry in Irish life, and vice versa. When Yeats summoned the literary and political figures (O' Leary, Standish O' Grady, Maud Gonne) associated with his past as 'All the Olympians; a thing never known again', the implicit judgment on the world he was soon to leave was quite clear. It did not measure up to *his* expectations and consequently, as he says in 'The Statues' (*Last Poems*):

> We Irish, born into that ancient sect
> But thrown upon this filthy modern tide
> And by its formless spawning fury wrecked,
> Climb to our proper dark, that we may trace
> The lineaments of a plummet-measured face.

Yeats's influence, both during his life and for some time after, was to elevate 'We Irish' into finding an appropriate place ('our proper dark') in the world which would, by example, reject the modern tide's 'formless spawning'. The impressive scope, idealistic ambition and imaginative demands of such a vision encouraged other poets, such as F.R. Higgins (1896-1941), unwisely to emulate it with little artistic success. Higgins's poet-friend, Austin Clarke (1896-1974) also started by imitating Yeats's epic range, then slowly and steadily realised after a period of artistic silence, bracketed by *Night and Morning* (1938) and *Ancient Lights* (1955) that the poet must follow his own imaginative light and not bask in one as powerful as Yeats's.

Patrick Kavanagh (1904-67), even at some remove, was greatly influenced by the cultural ideals and literary dominance of Yeats's writing. In some of his earlier work one hears the strain of Irish pastoralism which Yeats had promoted, but Kavanagh grew to despise 'Irishness' and rejected out-of-hand what he saw as the suffocating provincialism of the Irish literary scene, still caught in the spider's web of Yeats's writing or looking over its collective shoulder for approval to London.

While taking their roots from modernist poets Ezra Pound and T.S. Eliot, the artistic discipline of James Joyce, and drawing upon continental literary movements such as surrealism and on French poetry, the intellectual orientation of poets Denis Devlin (1908-59) and Brian Coffey (b.1905) had little in common with the pre-eminence of Yeats or his immediate poetic descendants. They sought, instead, to create a literature that was, in its sophistication and allusive concentration, free from overtly regional or national bearings.

Indeed, it could be said that with the death of Yeats and throughout the immediate aftermath of the Second World War, Ireland was cut off from the necessary wider cosmopolitan audience upon which poets like Coffey and Devlin depended. Ireland's policy of neutrality, however, confounded the English-based Northern Irish poet, Louis MacNeice (1907-63, who, incidentally, wrote a very fine book on Yeats in 1941) and drove a metaphorical wedge between the two parts of the country, reinforcing the seemingly different and contrasting paths Northern Ireland and the Republic of Ireland were to follow. This division strengthened the claims of poets such as John Hewitt (1907-87) in seeing the north of Ireland as a separate and distinctive region within the entire country, laying down the imaginative possibility in the 1940s and '50s for a renaissance of poetry in the province later on. When this actually did come about in the 1960s and '70s, the stimulus came not alone from

MacNeice and Hewitt, but included the vigorous self-awareness and colloquial manner of Patrick Kavanagh, who was brought up along the border in County Monaghan, and John Montague's (b.1929) reimagining of Ulster in global terms.

Roughly during this same period of the 1950s and '60s, the poetry of Thomas Kinsella (b.1928) was charting its own course, highly-mannered, austere and very conscious of the great changes in the writing of poetry which had taken place outside Ireland.

At the heart of what Richard Murphy (b.1927) writes, too, there is a troubled confrontation between past and present, but what marks out Murphy is the refined equipoise of his poetry, derived in part from his southern Anglo-Irish background and its inherited sense of being caught, or time-locked, between two worlds — at once grandly imperial but also marooned and decaying. This abiding tension, parallelling Yeats's, is finely contained by Murphy's formally distant, architectural designs, most noticeably in his collection, *The Price of Stone* (1985).

The precise *poetic* legacy of Yeats is to be found, however, in the style and structure of Derek Mahon's poetry. For Mahon, Belfast-born and from a Protestant background, has drawn imaginatively upon Yeats's 'big' stanzas, rigorously positioned syntax and rhetorical eloquence, most noticeably in a poem such as 'A Disused Shed in Co. Wexford'. However, Yeats's cultural nationalism has been rewritten and radicalised in the writings of Seamus Deane, poet-critic and driving force behind much of the publishing activity of Field Day, the Derry-based theatre company whose board includes poets Seamus Heaney and Tom Paulin, both of whom have engaged Yeats on an artistic and polemical level.

Of course, Yeats's influence has continued to bridge national boundaries, as well as generations, since W.H. Auden wrote his famous elegy, 'In Memory of W.B. Yeats' in 1939. American poets such as Theodore Roethke and John Berryman have noted the significance of Yeats in their own artistic lives; while one of England's most popular post-war poets, Philip Larkin, tells the story of his three years 'trying to write like Yeats, not because I liked his personality or understood his ideas but out of infatuation with his music'.

For quite different reasons too, what Larkin called Yeats's 'potent music' has also inspired African, Palestinian and South American writers who sought to give, in Seamus Deane's words, 'a voice and a history to those who have been deprived of both'. We should never discount this revolutionary example of Yeats's life and writing, in other words. Beyond which, artists and singer-songwriters from Van Morrison to Clannad and The Waterboys have heard in Yeats's work a sympathetic chord and fascinating vision.

∞

Yeats: A New Selection is designed to show not only the range of his poetry, but also how the artistic and the polemical crossed in Yeats's imagination. From the heady early lyrics and perfect imitations of ballads, to the passionate speech and architectural splendour of the sequences, the obsessions and self-doubts of his later work, Yeats's self-consciousness as a poet was always creatively deployed in the interest of *the poem*.

His imagination rested upon what literally surrounded him — the Irish countryside, which he saw so completely: the rural towns like Gort, the isolated districts like Ballylee, and the glorious beauty spots such as Ben Bulben and Innisfree. He imagined forests, streams, lakes, mountains as all having their own spirit which poetry could in some way embody. He heard the accents and rhetoric of street talk, committee rooms, clubs and the drawing rooms of The Big House, as well as the literary buzz of London and Paris, amongst other cities. He captured with individual flourish how ideals — of man, nature and nationalism — could be written out in verse. He could also see himself left alone without any illusions, 'caught in the cold snows of a dream'.

Yeats wrote about sexuality and love; about possible esoteric ways of understanding the world and about the materialistic drives that can take over people's lives unless they are very careful. He was, let there be no mistake about it, very much his own man. The story of his life is told in his poems as autobiography literally *becomes* art. For Yeats, though, the emphasis was always on dynamic transformation rather than passive self-confession.

This poetry should resonate with us today. For, like him, we battle away trying to find some kind of balance between experience and innocence, those contrary states which one of Yeats's greatest poetic and spiritual mentors, William Blake, powerfully dramatised in lyrical and prophetic verse.

Turning from the twentieth to the approaching twenty-first century, we can look back at Yeats making a similar journey between the nineteenth and twentieth. Where he saw England's industrialised democracy despoiling the green and pleasant land of Ireland, we, who are 'Green', see this worldwide struggle to preserve the natural bounty and ecological grace of the earth, threatened by either huge multinational conglomerates that tower over us or emasculated by theme-parks and heritage centres. As he heard and wrote out a new cultural notation for Irish self-perceptions, clouded and confused as they were by historical cross-signals, we too debate the meaning and viability of pluralism and national identity at a turbulent time of European federation. Where we look well beyond the institutions of religion for an understanding of life, he too experimented and explored other mystical sects like theosophy and spiritual practices from India. And in the conflicts of human friendship, companionship and love, Yeats was also there, sending back his report to whomever cared to listen.

Last, but by no means least, while we chivvy and demur about the role of the Artist, making too much or too little of what he or she can do at this turning of a new millennia, Yeats led by example — writing, campaigning, lecturing, touring, debating, organising and tirelessly giving of his energies (to the point of exhaustion) in what he believed was the artist's responsibility to his audience. This could well be Yeats's greatest legacy since he reminds us all now, writer and reader, performer and audience, that we are bound by the same rules of existence and when we set out to break them, we should know why. Yeats is the poet of limits *par excellence* telling us who we are, where we

come from and what we should try to become —
as individuals, as a nation and, indeed, as one
earth.

Yeats: A New Selection sets out to make available, in an inexpensive and handy edition, a reading of Yeats's lyrical poetry only; the narrative and dramatic verse can be found in the various collected editions. As an introduction, it should help the reader make up his or her own mind about one of the great modern masters of the English language.

Gerald Dawe
Galway, 1992

THE STOLEN CHILD

Where dips the rocky highland
Of Sleuth Wood in the lake,
There lies a leafy island
Where flapping herons wake
The drowsy water-rats;
There we've hid our faery vats,
Full of berries
And of reddest stolen cherries.
Come away, O human child!
To the waters and the wild
With a faery, hand in hand,
For the world's more full of weeping than you
can understand.

Where the wave of moonlight glosses
The dim grey sands with light,
Far off by furthest Rosses
We foot it all the night,
Weaving olden dances,
Mingling hands and mingling glances
Till the moon has taken flight;
To and fro we leap
And chase the frothy bubbles,

While the world is full of troubles
And is anxious in its sleep.
Come away, O human child!
To the waters and the wild
With a faery, hand in hand,
For the world's more full of weeping than you
can understand.

Where the wandering water gushes
From the hills above Glen-Car,
In pools among the rushes
That scarce could bathe a star.
We seek for slumbering trout
And whispering in their ears
Give them unquiet dreams;
Leaning softly out
From ferns that drop their tears
Over the young streams.
Come away, O human child!
To the waters and the wild
With a faery, hand in hand,
For the world's more full of weeping than you
can understand.

2

Away with us he's going,
The solemn-eyed:
He'll hear no more the lowing
Of the calves on the warm hillside
Or the kettle on the hob
Sing peace into his breast,
Or see the brown mice bob
Round and round the oatmeal-chest
For he comes, the human child,
To the waters and the wild
With a faery, hand in hand,
From a world more full of weeping than he
*   can understand.*

DOWN BY THE SALLEY GARDENS

Down by the salley gardens my love and I did meet;
She passed the salley gardens with little snow-white feet.
She bid me take love easy, as the leaves grow on the tree;
But I, being young and foolish, with her would not agree.

In a field by the river my love and I did stand,
And on my leaning shoulder she laid her snow-white hand.
She bid me take life easy, as the grass grows on the weirs;
But I was young and foolish, and now am full of tears.

THE BALLAD OF MOLL MAGEE

Come round me, little childer;
There, don't fling stones at me
Because I mutter as I go;
But pity Moll Magee.

My man was a poor fisher
With shore lines in the say;
My work was saltin' herrings
The whole of the long day.

And sometimes from the saltin' shed
I scarce could drag my feet,
Under the blessed moonlight,
Along the pebbly street.

I'd always been but weakly,
And my baby was just born;
A neighbour minded her by day,
I minded her till morn.

I lay upon my baby;
Ye little childer dear,
I looked upon my cold baby
When the morn grew frosty and clear.

A weary woman sleeps so hard!
My man grew red and pale,
And gave me money, and bade me go
To my own place, Kinsale.

He drove me out and shut the door,
And gave his curse to me;
I went away in silence,
No neighbour could I see.

The windows and the doors were shut,
One star shone faint and green,
The little straws were turnin' round
Across the bare boreen.

I went away in silence:
Beyond old Martin's byre
I saw a kindly neighbour
Blowin' her mornin' fire.

She drew from me my story —
My money's all used up,
And still, with pityin', scornin' eye,
She gives me bite and sup.

She says my man will surely come
And fetch me home agin;
But always, as I'm movin' round,
Without doors or within,

Pilin' the wood or pilin' the turf,
Or goin' to the well,
I'm thinkin' of my baby
And keenin' to mysel'.

And sometimes I am sure she knows
When, openin' wide His door,
God lights the stars, His candles,
And looks upon the poor.

So now, ye little childer,
Ye won't fling stones at me;
But gather with your shinin' looks
And pity Moll Magee.

CUCHULAIN'S FIGHT WITH THE SEA

A man came slowly from the setting sun,
To Emer, raddling raiment in her dun,
And said, 'I am that swineherd whom you bid
Go watch the road between the wood and tide,
But now I have no need to watch it more.'

Then Emer cast the web upon the floor,
And raising arms all raddled with the dye,
Parted her lips with a loud sudden cry.

That swineherd stared upon her face and said,
'No man alive, no man among the dead,
Has won the gold his cars of battle bring.'

'But if your master comes home triumphing
Why must you blench and shake from foot to crown?'

Thereon he shook the more and cast him down
Upon the web-heaped floor, and cried his word:
'With him is one sweet-throated like a bird.'

'You dare me to my face,' and thereupon
She smote with raddled fist, and where her son
Herded the cattle came with stumbling feet,
And cried with angry voice, 'It is not meet
To idle life away, a common herd.'

'I have long waited, mother, for that word:
But wherefore now?'

                    'There is a man to die;
You have the heaviest arm under the sky.'

'Whether under its daylight or its stars
My father stands amid his battle-cars.'

'But you have grown to be the taller man.'

'Yet somewhere under starlight or the sun
My father stands.'

                  'Aged, worn out with wars
On foot, on horseback or in battle-cars.'

'I only ask what way my journey lies,
For He who made you bitter made you wise.'

'The Red Branch camp in a great company
Between wood's rim and the horses of the sea.
Go there, and light a camp-fire at wood's rim;

But tell your name and lineage to him
Whose blade compels, and wait till they have found
Some feasting man that the same oath has bound.'

Among those feasting men Cuchulain dwelt,
And his young sweetheart close beside him knelt,
Stared on the mournful wonder of his eyes,
Even as Spring upon the ancient skies,
And pondered on the glory of his days;
And all around the harp-string told his praise,
And Conchubar, the Red Branch king of kings,
With his own fingers touched the brazen strings.

At last Cuchulain spake, 'Some man has made
His evening fire amid the leafy shade.
I have often heard him singing to and fro,
I have often heard the sweet sound of his bow.
Seek out what man he is.'

                         One went and came.
'He bade me let all know he gives his name
At the sword-point, and waits till we have found
Some feasting man that the same oath has bound.'

Cuchalain cried, 'I am the only man
Of all this host so bound from childhood on.'

After short fighting in the leafy shade,
He spake to the young man, 'Is there no maid
Who loves you, no white arms to wrap you round,
Or do you long for the dim sleepy ground,
That you have come and dared me to my face?'

'The dooms of men are in God's hidden place.'

'Your head a while seemed like a woman's head
That I loved once.'
               Again the fighting sped,
But now the war-rage in Cuchulain woke,
And through that new blade's guard the old blade broke,
And pierced him.
               'Speak before your breath is done.'

'Cuchulain I, mighty Cuchulain's son.'

'I put you from your pain. I can no more.'

While day its burden onto evening bore,
With head bowed on his knees Cuchulain stayed;
Then Conchubar sent that sweet-throated maid,
And she, to win him, his grey hair caressed;
In vain her arms, in vain her soft white breast.
Then Conchubar, the subtlest of all men,
Ranking his Druids round him ten by ten,

Spake thus: 'Cuchulain will dwell there and brood
For three days more in dreadful quietude,
And then arise, and raving slay us all.
Chaunt in his ear delusions magical,
That he may fight the horses of the sea.'
The Druids took them to their mystery,
And chaunted for three days.

                              Cuchulain stirred,
Stared on the horses of the sea, and heard
The cars of battle and his own name cried;
And fought with the invulnerable tide.

THE LAKE ISLE OF INNISFREE

I will arise and go now, and go to Innisfree,
And a small cabin build there, of clay and wattles made:
Nine bean-rows will I have there, a hive for the honey-bee,
And live alone in the bee-loud glade.

And I shall have some peace there, for peace comes
     dropping slow,
Dropping from the veils of the morning to where the
     cricket sings;
There midnight's all a glimmer, and noon a purple glow,
And evening full of the linnet's wings.

I will arise and go now, for always night and day
I hear lake water lapping with low sounds by the shore;
While I stand on the roadway, or on the pavements grey,
I hear it in the deep heart's core.

THE PITY OF LOVE

A pity beyond all telling
Is hid in the heart of love:
The folk who are buying and selling,
The clouds on their journey above,
The cold wet winds ever blowing,
And the shadowy hazel grove
Where mouse-grey waters are flowing,
Threaten the head that I love.

THE SORROW OF LOVE

The brawling of a sparrow in the eaves,
The brilliant moon and all the milky sky,
And all that famous harmony of leaves,
Had blotted out man's image and his cry.

A girl arose that had red mournful lips
And seemed the greatness of the world in tears,
Doomed like Odysseus and the labouring ships
And proud as Priam murdered with his peers;

Arose, and on the instant clamorous eaves,
A climbing moon upon an empty sky,
And all that lamentation of the leaves,
Could but compose man's image and his cry.

WHEN YOU ARE OLD

When you are old and grey and full of sleep,
And nodding by the fire, take down this book,
And slowly read, and dream of the soft look
Your eyes had once, and of their shadows deep;

How many loved your moments of glad grace,
And loved your beauty with love false or true,
But one man loved the pilgrim soul in you,
And loved the sorrows of your changing face;

And bending down beside the glowing bars,
Murmur, a little sadly, how Love fled
And paced upon the mountains overhead
And hid his face amid a crowd of stars.

THE MAN WHO DREAMED OF FAERYLAND

He stood among a crowd at Dromahair;
His heart hung all upon a silken dress,
And he had known at last some tenderness,
Before earth took him to her stony care;
But when a man poured fish into a pile,
It seemed they raised their little silver heads,
And sang what gold morning or evening sheds
Upon a woven world-forgotten isle
Where people love beside the ravelled seas;
That Time can never mar a lover's vows
Under that woven changeless roof of boughs:
The singing shook him out of his new ease.

He wandered by the sands of Lissadell;
His mind ran all on money cares and fears,
And he had known at last some prudent years
Before they heaped his grave under the hill;
But while he passed before a plashy place,
A lug-worm with its grey and muddy mouth
Sang that somewhere to north or west or south
There dwelt a gay, exulting, gentle race
Under the golden or the silver skies;
That if a dancer stayed his hungry foot
It seemed the sun and moon were in the fruit:
And at that singing he was no more wise.

He mused beside the well of Scanavin
He mused upon his mockers: without fail
His sudden vengeance were a country tale,
When earthy night had drunk his body in;
But one small knot-grass growing by the pool
Sang where — unnecessary cruel voice —
Old silence bids its chosen race rejoice,
Whatever ravelled waters rise and fall
Or stormy silver fret the gold of day,
And midnight there enfold them like a fleece
And lover there by lover be at peace.
The tale drove his fine angry mood away.

He slept under the hill of Lugnagall;
And might have known at last unhaunted sleep
Under that cold and vapour-turbaned steep,
Now that the earth had taken man and all:
Did not the worms that spired about his bones
Proclaim with that unwearied, reedy cry
That God has laid His fingers on the sky,
That from those fingers glittering summer runs
Upon the dancer by the dreamless wave.
Why should those lovers that no lovers miss
Dream, until God burn Nature with a kiss?
The man has found no comfort in the grave.

THE LAMENTATION OF THE OLD PENSIONER

Although I shelter from the rain
Under a broken tree,
My chair was nearest to the fire
In every company
That talked of love or politics,
Ere Time transfigured me.

Though lads are making pikes again
For some conspiracy,
And crazy rascals rage their fill
At human tyranny
My contemplations are of Time
That has transfigured me.

There's not a woman turns her face
Upon a broken tree,
And yet the beauties that I loved
Are in my memory;
I spit into the face of Time
That has transfigured me.

TO IRELAND IN THE COMING TIMES

Know, that I would accounted be
True brother of a company
That sang, to sweeten Ireland's wrong,
Ballad and story, rann and song;
Nor be I any less of them,
Because the red-rose-bordered hem
Of her, whose history began
Before God made the angelic clan,
Trails all about the written page.
When Time began to rant and rage
The measure of her flying feet
Made Ireland's heart begin to beat;
And Time bade all his candles flare
To light a measure here and there;
And may the thoughts of Ireland brood
Upon a measured quietude.

Nor may I less be counted one
With Davis, Mangan, Ferguson,
Because, to him who ponders well,
No rhymes more than their rhyming tell
Of things discovered in the deep,
Where only body's laid asleep.
For the elemental creatures go

About my table to and fro,
That hurry from unmeasured mind
To rant and rage in flood and wind;
Yet he who treads in measured ways
May surely barter gaze for gaze.
Man ever journeys on with them
After the red-rose-bordered hem.
Ah, faeries, dancing under the moon,
A Druid land, a Druid tune!

While still I may, I write for you
The love I lived, the dream I knew.
From our birthday, until we die,
Is but the winking of an eye;
And we, our singing and our love,
What measurer Time has lit above,
And all benighted things that go
About my table to and fro,
Are passing on to where may be,
In truth's consuming ecstasy,
No place for love and dream at all;
For God goes by with white footfall.
I cast my heart into my rhymes,
That you, in the dim coming times,
May know how my heart went with them
After the red-rose-bordered hem.

THE FISH

Although you hide in the ebb and flow
Of the pale tide when the moon has set,
The people of coming days will know
About the casting out of my net,

And how you have leaped times out of mind
Over the little silver cords,
And think that you were hard and unkind,
And blame you with many bitter words.

THE SONG OF WANDERING AENGUS

I went out to the hazel wood,
Because a fire was in my head,
And cut and peeled a hazel wand,
And hooked a berry to a thread;
And when white moths were on the wing,
And moth-like stars were flickering out,
I dropped the berry in a stream
And caught a little silver trout.

When I had laid it on the floor
I went to blow the fire aflame,
But something rustled on the floor,
And some one called me by my name:
It had become a glimmering girl
With apple blossom in her hair
Who called me by my name and ran
And faded through the brightening air.

Though I am old with wandering
Through hollow lands and hilly lands,
I will find out where she has gone,
And kiss her lips and take her hands;
And walk among long dappled grass,
And pluck till time and times are done
The silver apples of the moon,
The golden apples of the sun.

HE BIDS HIS BELOVED BE AT PEACE

I hear the Shadowy Horses, their long manes a-shake,
Their hoofs heavy with tumult, their eyes glimmering white;
The North unfolds above them clinging, creeping night,
The East her hidden joy before the morning break,
The West weeps in pale dew and sighs passing away,
The South is pouring down roses of crimson fire:
O vanity of Sleep, Hope, Dream, endless Desire,
The Horses of Disaster plunge in the heavy clay:
Beloved, let your eyes half close, and your heart beat
Over my heart, and your hair fall over my breast,
Drowning love's lonely hour in deep twilight of rest,
And hiding their tossing manes and their tumultuous feet.

THE CAP AND BELLS

The jester walked in the garden:
The garden had fallen still;
He bade his soul rise upward
And stand on her window-sill.

It rose in a straight blue garment,
When owls began to call:
It had grown wise-tongued by thinking
Of a quiet and light footfall;

But the young queen would not listen;
She rose in her pale night-gown;
She drew in the heavy casement
And pushed the latches down.

He bade his heart go to her,
When the owls called out no more;
In a red and quivering garment
It sang to her through the door.

It had grown sweet-tongued by dreaming
Of a flutter of flower-like hair;
But she took up her fan from the table
And waved it off on the air.

'I have cap and bells,' he pondered,
'I will send them to her and die';
And when the morning whitened
He left them where she went by.

She laid them upon her bosom,
Under a cloud of her hair,
And her red lips sang them a love-song
Till stars grew out of the air.

She opened her door and her window,
And the heart and the soul came through,
To her right hand came the red one,
To her left hand came the blue.

They set up a noise like crickets,
A chattering wise and sweet,
And her hair was a folded flower
And the quiet of love in her feet.

THE VALLEY OF THE BLACK PIG

The dews drop slowly and dreams gather: unknown spears
Suddenly hurtle before my dream-awakened eyes,
And then the clash of fallen horsemen and the cries
Of unknown perishing armies beat about my ears.
We who still labour by the cromlech on the shore,
The grey cairn on the hill, when day sinks drowned in
  dew,
Being weary of the world's empires, bow down to you,
Master of the still stars and of the flaming door.

THE LOVER PLEADS WITH HIS FRIEND
FOR OLD FRIENDS

Though you are in your shining days,
Voices among the crowd
And new friends busy with your praise,
Be not unkind or proud,
But think about old friends the most:
Time's bitter flood will rise,
Your beauty perish and be lost
For all eyes but these eyes.

HE WISHES FOR THE CLOTHS OF HEAVEN

Had I the heavens' embroidered cloths,
Enwrought with golden and silver light,
The blue and the dim and the dark cloths
Of night and light and the half-light,
I would spread the cloths under your feet:
But I, being poor, have only my dreams;
I have spread my dreams under your feet;
Tread softly because you tread on my dreams.

THE FIDDLER OF DOONEY

When I play on my fiddle in Dooney,
Folk dance like a wave of the sea;
My cousin is priest in Kilvarnet,
My brother in Mocharabuiee.

I passed my brother and cousin:
They read in their books of prayer;
I read in my book of songs
I bought at the Sligo fair.

When we come at the end of time
To Peter sitting in state,
He will smile on the three old spirits,
But call me first through the gate;

For the good are always the merry,
Save by an evil chance,
And the merry love the fiddle,
And the merry love to dance:

And when the folk there spy me,
They will all come up to me,
With 'Here is the fiddler of Dooney!'
And dance like a wave of the sea.

IN THE SEVEN WOODS

I have heard the pigeons of the Seven Woods
Make their faint thunder, and the garden bees
Hum in the lime-tree flowers: and put away
The unavailing outcries and the old bitterness
That empty the heart. I have forgot awhile
Tara uprooted, and new commonness
Upon the throne and crying about the streets
And hanging its paper flowers from post to post,
Because it is alone of all things happy.
I am contented, for I know that Quiet
Wanders laughing and eating her wild heart
Among pigeons and bees, while that Great Archer,
Who but awaits His hour to shoot, still hangs
A cloudy quiver over Pairc-na-lee.

August 1902

NEVER GIVE ALL THE HEART

Never give all the heart, for love
Will hardly seem worth thinking of
To passionate women if it seem
Certain, and they never dream
That it fades out from kiss to kiss;
For everything that's lovely is
But a brief, dreamy, kind delight.
O never give the heart outright,
For they, for all smooth lips can say,
Have given their hearts up to the play.
And who could play it well enough
If deaf and dumb and blind with love?
He that made this knows all the cost,
For he gave all his heart and lost.

NO SECOND TROY

Why should I blame her that she filled my days
With misery, or that she would of late
Have taught to ignorant men most violent ways,
Or hurled the little streets upon the great,
Had they but courage equal to desire?
What could have made her peaceful with a mind
That nobleness made simple as a fire,
With beauty like a tightened bow, a kind
That is not natural in an age like this,
Being high and solitary and most stern?
Why, what could she have done, being what she is?
Was there another Troy for her to burn?

RECONCILIATION

Some may have blamed you that you took away
The verses that could move them on the day
When, the ears being deafened, the sight of the eyes blind
With lightning, you went from me, and I could find
Nothing to make a song about but kings,
Helmets, and swords, and half-forgotten things
That were like memories of you — but now
We'll out, for the world lives as long ago;
And while we're in our laughing, weeping fit,
Hurl helmets, crowns, and swords into the pit.
But, dear, cling close to me; since you were gone,
My barren thoughts have chilled me to the bone.

THE FASCINATION OF WHAT'S DIFFICULT

The fascination of what's difficult
Has dried the sap out of my veins, and rent
Spontaneous joy and natural content
Out of my heart. There's something ails our colt
That must, as if it had not holy blood
Nor on Olympus leaped from cloud to cloud,
Shiver under the lash, strain, sweat and jolt
As though it dragged road-metal. My curse on plays
That have to be set up in fifty ways,
On the day's war with every knave and dolt,
Theatre business, management of men.
I swear before the dawn comes round again
I'll find the stable and pull out the bolt.

ON HEARING THAT THE STUDENTS OF OUR NEW UNIVERSITY HAVE JOINED THE AGITATION AGAINST IMMORAL LITERATURE

Where, where but here have Pride and Truth,
That long to give themselves for wage,
To shake their wicked sides at youth
Restraining reckless middle-age?

AT THE ABBEY THEATRE

(Imitated from Ronsard)

Dear Craoibhin Aoibhin, look into our case.
When we are high and airy hundreds say
That if we hold that flight they'll leave the place,
While those same hundreds mock another day
Because we have made our art of common things,
So bitterly, you'd dream they longed to look
All their lives through into some drift of wings.
You've dandled them and fed them from the book
And know them to the bone; impart to us —
We'll keep the secret — a new trick to please.
Is there a bridle for this Proteus
That turns and changes like his draughty seas?
Or is there none, most popular of men,
But when they mock us, that we mock again?

ALL THINGS CAN TEMPT ME

All things can tempt me from this craft of verse:
One time it was a woman's face, or worse —
The seeming needs of my fool-driven land;
Now nothing but comes readier to the hand
Than this accustomed toil. When I was young,
I had not given a penny for a song
Did not the poet sing it with such airs
That one believed he had a sword upstairs;
Yet would be now, could I but have my wish,
Colder and dumber and deafer than a fish.

TO A WEALTHY MAN WHO PROMISED A SECOND SUBSCRIPTION TO THE DUBLIN MUNICIPAL GALLERY IF IT WERE PROVED THE PEOPLE WANTED PICTURES

You gave, but will not give again
Until enough of Paudeen's pence
By Biddy's halfpennies have lain
To be 'some sort of evidence',
Before you'll put your guineas down,
That things it were a pride to give
Are what the blind and ignorant town
Imagines best to make it thrive.
What cared Duke Ercole, that bid
His mummers to the market-place,
What th' onion-sellers thought or did
So that his Plautus set the pace
For the Italian comedies?
And Guidobaldo, when he made
That grammar school of courtesies
Where wit and beauty learned their trade
Upon Urbino's windy hill,
Had sent no runners to and fro
That he might learn the shepherds' will.
And when they drove out Cosimo,

Indifferent how the rancour ran,
He gave the hours they had set free
To Michelozzo's latest plan
For the San Marco Library,
Whence turbulent Italy should draw
Delight in Art whose end is peace,
In logic and in natural law
By sucking at the dugs of Greece.

Your open hand but shows our loss,
For he knew better how to live.
Let Paudeens play at pitch and toss,
Look up in the sun's eye and give
What the exultant heart calls good
That some new day may breed the best
Because you gave, not what they would,
But the right twigs for an eagle's nest!

December 1912

SEPTEMBER 1913

What need you, being come to sense,
But fumble in a greasy till
And add the halfpence to the pence
And prayer to shivering prayer, until
You have dried the marrow from the bone?
For men were born to pray and save:
Romantic Ireland's dead and gone,
It's with O'Leary in the grave.

Yet they were of a different kind,
The names that stilled your childish play,
They have gone about the world like wind,
But little time had they to pray
For whom the hangman's rope was spun,
And what, God help us, could they save?
Romantic Ireland's dead and gone,
It's with O'Leary in the grave.

Was it for this the wild geese spread
The grey wing upon every tide;
For this that all that blood was shed,
For this Edward Fitzgerald died,
And Robert Emmet and Wolfe Tone,
All that delirium of the brave?
Romantic Ireland's dead and gone,
It's with O'Leary in the grave.

Yet could we turn the years again,
And call those exiles as they were
In all their loneliness and pain,
You'd cry, 'Some woman's yellow hair
Has maddened every mother's son':
They weighed so lightly what they gave.
But let them be, they're dead and gone,
They're with O'Leary in the grave.

PAUDEEN

Indignant at the fumbling wits, the obscure spite
Of our old Paudeen in his shop, I stumbled blind
Among the stones and thorn-trees, under morning light;
Until a curlew cried and in the luminous wind
A curlew answered; and suddenly thereupon I thought
That on the lonely height where all are in God's eye,
There cannot be, confusion of our sound forgot,
A single soul that lacks a sweet crystalline cry.

ON THOSE THAT HATED 'THE PLAYBOY OF THE WESTERN WORLD', 1907

Once, when midnight smote the air,
Eunuchs ran through Hell and met
On every crowded street to stare
Upon great Juan riding by:
Even like these to rail and sweat
Staring upon his sinewy thigh.

THE REALISTS

Hope that you may understand!
What can books of men that wive
In a dragon-guarded land,
Paintings of the dolphin-drawn
Sea-nymphs in their pearly wagons
Do, but awake a hope to live
That had gone
With the dragons?

FRIENDS

Now must I these three praise —
Three women that have wrought
What joy is in my days:
One because no thought,
Nor those unpassing cares,
No, not in these fifteen
Many-times-troubled years,
Could ever come between
Mind and delighted mind;
And one because her hand
Had strength that could unbind
What none can understand,
What none can have and thrive,
Youth's dreamy load, till she
So changed me that I live
Labouring in ecstasy.
And what of her that took
All till my youth was gone
With scarce a pitying look?
How could I praise that one?
When day begins to break
I count my good and bad,
Being wakeful for her sake,

Remembering what she had,
What eagle look still shows,
While up from my heart's root
So great a sweetness flows
I shake from head to foot.

THE COLD HEAVEN

Suddenly I saw the cold and rook-delighting heaven
That seemed as though ice burned and was but the more ice,
And thereupon imagination and heart were driven
So wild that every casual thought of that and this
Vanished, and left but memories, that should be out of season
With the hot blood of youth, of love crossed long ago;
And I took all the blame out of all sense and reason,
Until I cried and trembled and rocked to and fro,
Riddled with light. Ah! when the ghost begins to quicken,
Confusion of the death-bed over, is it sent
Out naked on the roads, as the books say, and stricken
By the injustice of the skies for punishment?

AN APPOINTMENT

Being out of heart with government
I took a broken root to fling
Where the proud, wayward squirrel went,
Taking delight that he could spring;
And he, with that low whinnying sound
That is like laughter, sprang again
And so to the other tree at a bound.
Nor the tame will, nor timid brain,
Nor heavy knitting of the brow
Bred that fierce tooth and cleanly limb
And threw him up to laugh on the bough:
No government appointed him.

A COAT

I made my song a coat
Covered with embroideries
Out of old mythologies
From heel to throat;
But the fools caught it,
Wore it in the world's eyes
As though they'd wrought it.
Song, let them take it,
For there's more enterprise
In walking naked.

THE WILD SWANS AT COOLE

The trees are in their autumn beauty,
The woodland paths are dry,
Under the October twilight the water
Mirrors a still sky;
Upon the brimming water among the stones
Are nine-and-fifty swans.

The nineteenth autumn has come upon me
Since I first made my count;
I saw, before I had well finished,
All suddenly mount
And scatter wheeling in great broken rings
Upon their clamorous wings.

I have looked upon those brilliant creatures,
And now my heart is sore.
All's changed since I, hearing at twilight,
The first time on this shore,
The bell-beat of their wings above my head,
Trod with a lighter tread.

Unwearied still, lover by lover,
They paddle in the cold
Companionable streams or climb the air;
Their hearts have not grown old;
Passion or conquest, wander where they will,
Attend upon them still.

But now they drift on the still water,
Mysterious, beautiful;
Among what rushes will they build,
By what lake's edge or pool
Delight men's eyes when I awake some day
To find they have flown away?

AN IRISH AIRMAN FORESEES HIS DEATH

I know that I shall meet my fate
Somewhere among the clouds above;
Those that I fight I do not hate,
Those that I guard I do not love;
My country is Kiltartan Cross,
My countrymen Kiltartan's poor,
No likely end could bring them loss
Or leave them happier than before.
Nor law, nor duty bade me fight,
Nor public men, nor cheering crowds,
A lonely impulse of delight
Drove to this tumult in the clouds;
I balanced all, brought all to mind,
The years to come seemed waste of breath,
A waste of breath the years behind
In balance with this life, this death.

TO A YOUNG BEAUTY

Dear fellow-artist, why so free
With every sort of company,
With every Jack and Jill?
Choose your companions from the best;
Who draws a bucket with the rest
Soon topples down the hill.

You may, that mirror for a school,
Be passionate, not bountiful
As common beauties may,
Who were not born to keep in trim
With old Ezekiel's cherubim
But those of Beauvarlet.

I know what wages beauty gives,
How hard a life her servant lives,
Yet praise the winters gone:
There is not a fool can call me friend,
And I may dine at journey's end
With Landor and with Donne.

THE SCHOLARS

Bald heads forgetful of their sins,
Old, learned, respectable bald heads
Edit and annotate the lines
That young men, tossing on their beds,
Rhymed out in love's despair
To flatter beauty's ignorant ear.

All shuffle there; all cough in ink;
All wear the carpet with their shoes;
All think what other people think;
All know the man their neighbour knows.
Lord, what would they say
Did their Catullus walk that way?

THE FISHERMAN

Although I can see him still,
The freckled man who goes
To a grey place on a hill
In grey Connemara clothes
At dawn to cast his flies,
It's long since I began
To call up to the eyes
This wise and simple man.
All day I'd looked in the face
What I had hoped 'twould be
To write for my own race
And the reality;
The living men that I hate,
The dead man that I loved,
The craven man in his seat,
The insolent unreproved,
And no knave brought to book
Who has won a drunken cheer,
The witty man and his joke
Aimed at the commonest ear,

The clever man who cries
The catch-cries of the clown,
The beating down of the wise
And great Art beaten down.

Maybe a twelvemonth since
Suddenly I began,
In scorn of this audience,
Imagining a man,
And his sun-freckled face,
And grey Connemara cloth,
Climbing up to a place
Where stone is dark under froth,
And the down-turn of his wrist
When the flies drop in the stream;
A man who does not exist,
A man who is but a dream;
And cried, 'Before I am old
I shall have written him one
Poem maybe as cold
And passionate as the dawn.'

THE PEOPLE

'What have I earned for all that work,' I said,
'For all that I have done at my own charge?
The daily spite of this unmannerly town,
Where who has served the most is most defamed,
The reputation of his lifetime lost
Between the night and morning. I might have lived,
And you know well how great the longing has been,
Where every day my footfall should have lit
In the green shadow of Ferrara wall;
Or climbed among the images of the past —
The unperturbed and courtly images —
Evening and morning, the steep street of Urbino
To where the Duchess and her people talked
The stately midnight through until they stood
In their great window looking at the dawn;
I might have had no friend that could not mix
Courtesy and passion into one like those
That saw the wicks grow yellow in the dawn;
I might have used the one substantial right
My trade allows: chosen my company,
And chosen what scenery had pleased me best.'
Thereon my phoenix answered in reproof,
'The drunkards, pilferers of public funds,

All the dishonest crowd I had driven away,
When my luck changed and they dared meet my face,
Crawled from obscurity, and set upon me
Those I had served and some that I had fed;
Yet never have I, now nor any time,
Complained of the people.'

                      All I could reply
Was: 'You, that have not lived in thought but deed,
Can have the purity of a natural force,
But I, whose virtues are the definitions
Of the analytic mind, can neither close
The eye of the mind nor keep my tongue from speech.'
And yet, because my heart leaped at her words,
I was abashed, and now they come to mind
After nine years, I sink my head abashed.

BROKEN DREAMS

There is grey in your hair.
Young men no longer suddenly catch their breath
When you are passing;
But maybe some old gaffer mutters a blessing
Because it was your prayer
Recovered him upon the bed of death.
For your sole sake — that all heart's ache have known,
And given to others all heart's ache,
From meagre girlhood's putting on
Burdensome beauty — for your sole sake
Heaven has put away the stroke of her doom,
So great her portion in that peace you make
By merely walking in a room.

Your beauty can but leave among us
Vague memories, nothing but memories.
A young man when the old men are done talking
Will say to an old man, 'Tell me of that lady
The poet stubborn with his passion sang us
When age might well have chilled his blood.'

Vague memories, nothing but memories,
But in the grave all, all, shall be renewed.
The certainty that I shall see that lady
Leaning or standing or walking
In the first loveliness of womanhood,
And with the fervour of my youthful eyes,
Has set me muttering like a fool.

You are more beautiful than any one,
And yet your body had a flaw:
Your small hands were not beautiful,
And I am afraid that you will run
And paddle to the wrist
In that mysterious, always brimming lake
Where those that have obeyed the holy law
Paddle and are perfect. Leave unchanged
The hands that I have kissed,
For old sake's sake.

The last stroke of midnight dies.
All day in the one chair
From dream to dream and rhyme to rhyme I have ranged
In rambling talk with an image of air:
Vague memories, nothing but memories.

ON BEING ASKED FOR A WAR POEM

I think it better that in times like these
A poet's mouth be silent, for in truth
We have no gift to set a statesman right;
He has had enough of meddling who can please
A young girl in the indolence of her youth,
Or an old man upon a winter's night.

EGO DOMINUS TUUS

Hic. On the grey sand beside the shallow stream
  Under your old wind-beaten tower, where still
  A lamp burns on beside the open book
  That Michael Robartes left, you walk in the moon,
  And, though you have passed the best of life, still trace,
  Enthralled by the unconquerable delusion,
  Magical shapes.

Ille.   By the help of an image
  I call to my own opposite, summon all
  That I have handled least, least looked upon.

Hic. And I would find myself and not an image.

Ille. That is our modern hope, and by its light
  We have lit upon the gentle, sensitive mind
  And lost the old nonchalance of the hand;
  Whether we have chosen chisel, pen or brush,
  We are but critics, or but half create,
  Timid, entangled, empty and abashed,
  Lacking the countenance of our friends.

Hic.   And yet

    The chief imagination of Christendom,
    Dante Alighieri, so utterly found himself
    That he has made that hollow face of his
    More plain to the mind's eye than any face
    But that of Christ.

Ille.   And did he find himself

    Or was the hunger that had made it hollow
    A hunger for the apple on the bough
    Most out of reach? and is that spectral image
    The man that Lapo and that Guido knew?
    I think he fashioned from his opposite
    An image that might have been a stony face
    Staring upon a Bedouin's horse-hair roof
    From doored and windowed cliff, or half upturned
    Among the coarse grass and the camel-dung.
    He set his chisel to the hardest stone.
    Being mocked by Guido for his lecherous life,
    Derided and deriding, driven out
    To climb that stair and eat that bitter bread,
    He found the unpersuadable justice, he found
    The most exalted lady loved by a man.

Hic. Yet surely there are men who have made their art
   Out of no tragic war, lovers of life,
   Impulsive men that look for happiness
   And sing when they have found it.

Ille.   No, not sing,
   For those that love the world serve it in action:
   Grow rich, popular and full of influence,
   And should they paint or write, still it is action;
   The struggle of the fly in marmalade.
   The rhetorician would deceive his neighbours,
   The sentimentalist himself; while art
   Is but a vision of reality.
   What portion in the world can the artist have
   Who has awakened from the common dream
   But dissipation and despair?

Hic.   And yet
   No one denies to Keats love of the world;
   Remember his deliberate happiness.

Ille. His art is happy, but who knows his mind?
   I see a schoolboy when I think of him,
   With face and nose pressed to a sweet-shop window,
   For certainly he sank into his grave
   His senses and his heart unsatisfied,

And made — being poor, ailing and ignorant,
Shut out from all the luxury of the world,
The coarse-bred son of a livery-stable keeper —
Luxuriant song.

Hic.   Why should you leave the lamp
Burning alone beside an open book,
And trace these characters upon the sands?
A style is found by sedentary toil
And by the imitation of great masters.

Ille. Because I seek an image, not a book.
Those men that in their writings are most wise
Own nothing but their blind, stupefied hearts.
I call to the mysterious one who yet
Shall walk the wet sands by the edge of the stream
And look most like me, being indeed my double,
And prove of all imaginable things
The most unlike, being my anti-self,
And, standing by these characters, disclose
All that I seek; and whisper it as though
He were afraid the birds, who cry aloud
Their momentary cries before it is dawn,
Would carry it away to blasphemous men.

A PRAYER ON GOING INTO MY HOUSE

God grant a blessing on this tower and cottage
And on my heirs, if all remain unspoiled,
No table or chair or stool not simple enough
For shepherd lads in Galilee; and grant
That I myself for portions of the year
May handle nothing and set eyes on nothing
But what the great and passionate have used
Throughout so many varying centuries
We take it for the norm; yet should I dream
Sinbad the sailor's brought a painted chest,
Or image, from beyond the Loadstone Mountain,
That dream is a norm; and should some limb of the Devil
Destroy the view by cutting down an ash
That shades the road, or setting up a cottage
Planned in a government office, shorten his life,
Manacle his soul upon the Red Sea bottom.

THE CAT AND THE MOON

The cat went here and there
And the moon spun round like a top,
And the nearest kin of the moon,
The creeping cat, looked up.
Black Minnaloushe stared at the moon,
For, wander and wail as he would,
The pure cold light in the sky
Troubled his animal blood.
Minnaloushe runs in the grass
Lifting his delicate feet.
Do you dance, Minnaloushe, do you dance?
When two close kindred meet,
What better than call a dance?
Maybe the moon may learn,
Tired of that courtly fashion,
A new dance turn.
Minnaloushe creeps through the grass
From moonlit place to place,
The sacred moon overhead
Has taken a new phase.
Does Minnaloushe know that his pupils
Will pass from change to change,
And that from round to crescent,

From crescent to round they range?
Minnaloushe creeps through the grass
Alone, important and wise,
And lifts to the changing moon
His changing eyes.

UNDER SATURN

Do not because this day I have grown saturnine
Imagine that lost love, inseparable from my thought
Because I have no other youth, can make me pine;
For how should I forget the wisdom that you brought,
The comfort that you made? Although my wits have gone
On a fantastic ride, my horse's flanks are spurred
By childish memories of an old cross Pollexfen,
And of a Middleton, whose name you never heard,
And of a red-haired Yeats whose looks, although he died
Before my time, seem like a vivid memory.
You heard that labouring man who had served my people.
      He said
Upon the open road, near to the Sligo quay —
No, no, not said, but cried it out — 'You have come again,
And surely after twenty years it was time to come.'
I am thinking of a child's vow sworn in vain
Never to leave that valley his fathers called their home.

November 1919

EASTER 1916

I have met them at close of day
Coming with vivid faces
From counter or desk among grey
Eighteenth-century houses.
I have passed with a nod of the head
Or polite meaningless words,
Or have lingered awhile and said
Polite meaningless words,
And thought before I had done
Of a mocking tale or a gibe
To please a companion
Around the fire at the club,
Being certain that they and I
But lived where motley is worn:
All changed, changed utterly:
A terrible beauty is born.

That woman's days were spent
In ignorant good-will,
Her nights in argument
Until her voice grew shrill.
What voice more sweet than hers
When, young and beautiful,

She rode to harriers?
This man had kept a school
And rode our wingèd horse;
This other his helper and friend
Was coming into his force;
He might have won fame in the end,
So sensitive his nature seemed,
So daring and sweet his thought.
This other man I had dreamed
A drunken, vainglorious lout.
He had done most bitter wrong
To some who are near my heart,
Yet I number him in the song;
He, too, has resigned his part
In the casual comedy;
He, too, has been changed in his turn,
Transformed utterly:
A terrible beauty is born.

Hearts with one purpose alone
Through summer and winter seem
Enchanted to a stone
To trouble the living stream.
The horse that comes from the road,
The rider, the birds that range
From cloud to tumbling cloud,
Minute by minute they change;

A shadow of cloud on the stream
Changes minute by minute;
A horse-hoof slides on the brim,
And a horse plashes within it;
The long-legged moor-hens dive,
And hens to moor-cocks call;
Minute by minute they live:
The stone's in the midst of all.

Too long a sacrifice
Can make a stone of the heart.
O when may it suffice?
That is Heaven's part, our part
To murmur name upon name,
As a mother names her child
When sleep at last has come
On limbs that had run wild.
What is it but nightfall?
No, no, not night but death;
Was it needless death after all?
For England may keep faith
For all that is done and said.
We know their dream; enough
To know they dreamed and are dead;
And what if excess of love
Bewildered them till they died?
I write it out in a verse —

MacDonagh and MacBride
And Connolly and Pearse
Now and in time to be,
Wherever green is worn,
Are changed, changed utterly:
A terrible beauty is born.

September 25, 1916

SIXTEEN DEAD MEN

O but we talked at large before
The sixteen men were shot,
But who can talk of give and take,
What should be and what not
While those dead men are loitering there
To stir the boiling pot?

You say that we should still the land
Till Germany's overcome;
But who is there to argue that
Now Pearse is deaf and dumb?
And is their logic to outweigh
MacDonagh's bony thumb?

How could you dream they'd listen
That have an ear alone
For those new comrades they have found,
Lord Edward and Wolfe Tone,
Or meddle with our give and take
That converse bone to bone?

THE ROSE TREE

'O words are lightly spoken,'
Said Pearse to Connolly,
'Maybe a breath of politic words
Has withered our Rose Tree;
Or maybe but a wind that blows
Across the bitter sea.'

'It needs to be but watered,'
James Connolly replied,
'To make the green come out again
And spread on every side,
And shake the blossom from the bud
To be the garden's pride.'

'But where can we draw water,'
Said Pearse to Connolly,
'When all the wells are parched away?
O plain as plain can be
There's nothing but our own red blood
Can make a right Rose Tree.'

THE SECOND COMING

Turning and turning in the widening gyre
The falcon cannot hear the falconer;
Things fall apart; the centre cannot hold;
Mere anarchy is loosed upon the world,
The blood-dimmed tide is loosed, and everywhere
The ceremony of innocence is drowned;
The best lack all conviction, while the worst
Are full of passionate intensity.

Surely some revelation is at hand;
Surely the Second Coming is at hand.
The Second Coming! Hardly are those words out
When a vast image out of *Spiritus Mundi*
Troubles my sight: somewhere in sands of the desert
A shape with lion body and the head of a man,
A gaze blank and pitiless as the sun,
Is moving its slow thighs, while all about it
Reel shadows of the indignant desert birds.
The darkness drops again; but now I know
That twenty centuries of stony sleep
Were vexed to nightmare by a rocking cradle,
And what rough beast, its hour come round at last,
Slouches towards Bethlehem to be born?

A PRAYER FOR MY DAUGHTER

Once more the storm is howling, and half hid
Under this cradle-hood and coverlid
My child sleeps on. There is no obstacle
But Gregory's wood and one bare hill
Whereby the haystack-and roof-levelling wind,
Bred on the Atlantic, can be stayed;
And for an hour I have walked and prayed
Because of the great gloom that is in my mind.

I have walked and prayed for this young child an hour
And heard the sea-wind scream upon the tower,
And under the arches of the bridge, and scream
In the elms above the flooded stream;
Imagining in excited reverie
That the future years had come,
Dancing to a frenzied drum,
Out of the murderous innocence of the sea.

May she be granted beauty and yet not
Beauty to make a stranger's eye distraught,
Or hers before a looking-glass, for such,
Being made beautiful overmuch,
Consider beauty a sufficient end,

Lose natural kindness and maybe
The heart-revealing intimacy
That chooses right, and never find a friend.

Helen being chosen found life flat and dull
And later had much trouble from a fool,
While that great Queen, that rose out of the spray,
Being fatherless could have her way
Yet chose a bandy-leggèd smith for man.
It's certain that fine women eat
A crazy salad with their meat
Whereby the Horn of Plenty is undone.

In courtesy I'd have her chiefly learned;
Hearts are not had as a gift but hearts are earned
By those that are not entirely beautiful;
Yet many, that have played the fool
For beauty's very self, has charm made wise,
And many a poor man that has roved,
Loved and thought himself beloved,
From a glad kindness cannot take his eyes.

May she become a flourishing hidden tree
That all her thoughts may like the linnet be,
And have no business but dispensing round
Their magnanimities of sound,
Nor but in merriment begin a chase,

Nor but in merriment a quarrel.
O may she live like some green laurel
Rooted in one dear perpetual place.

My mind, because the minds that I have loved,
The sort of beauty that I have approved,
Prosper but little, has dried up of late,
Yet knows that to be choked with hate
May well be of all evil chances chief.
If there's no hatred in a mind
Assault and battery of the wind
Can never tear the linnet from the leaf.

An intellectual hatred is the worst,
So let her think opinions are accursed.
Have I not seen the loveliest woman born
Out of the mouth of Plenty's horn,
Because of her opinionated mind
Barter that horn and every good
By quiet natures understood
For an old bellows full of angry wind?

Considering that, all hatred driven hence,
The soul recovers radical innocence
And learns at last that it is self-delighting,
Self-appeasing, self-affrighting,
And that its own sweet will is Heaven's will;

She can, though every face should scowl
And every windy quarter howl
Or every bellows burst, be happy still.

And may her bridegroom bring her to a house
Where all's accustomed, ceremonious;
For arrogance and hatred are the wares
Peddled in the thoroughfares.
How but in custom and in ceremony
Are innocence and beauty born?
Ceremony's a name for the rich horn,
And custom for the spreading laurel tree.

June 1919

TO BE CARVED ON A STONE AT THOOR BALLYLEE

I, the poet William Yeats,
With old mill boards and sea-green slates,
And smithy work from the Gort forge,
Restored this tower for my wife George;
And may these characters remain
When all is ruin once again.

SAILING TO BYZANTIUM

I

That is no country for old men. The young
In one another's arms, birds in the trees
— Those dying generations — at their song,
The salmon-falls, the mackerel-crowded seas,
Fish, flesh, or fowl, commend all summer long
Whatever is begotten, born, and dies.
Caught in that sensual music all neglect
Monuments of unageing intellect.

II

An aged man is but a paltry thing,
A tattered coat upon a stick, unless
Soul clap its hands and sing, and louder sing
For every tatter in its mortal dress,
Nor is there singing school but studying
Monuments of its own magnificence;
And therefore I have sailed the seas and come
To the holy city of Byzantium.

III

O sages standing in God's holy fire
As in the gold mosaic of a wall,
Come from the holy fire, perne in a gyre,
And be the singing-masters of my soul.
Consume my heart away; sick with desire
And fastened to a dying animal
It knows not what it is; and gather me
Into the artifice of eternity.

IV

Once out of nature I shall never take
My bodily form from any natural thing,
But such a form as Grecian goldsmiths make
Of hammered gold and gold enamelling
To keep a drowsy Emperor awake;
Or set upon a golden bough to sing
To lords and ladies of Byzantium
Of what is past, or passing, or to come.

1927

MEDITATIONS IN TIME OF CIVIL WAR

II

My House

An ancient bridge, and a more ancient tower,
A farmhouse that is sheltered by its wall,
An acre of stony ground,
Where the symbolic rose can break in flower,
Old ragged elms, old thorns innumerable,
The sound of the rain or sound
Of every wind that blows;
The stilted water-hen
Crossing stream again
Scared by the splashing of a dozen cows;

A winding stair, a chamber arched with stone,
A grey stone fireplace with an open hearth,
A candle and written page.
Il Penseroso's Platonist toiled on
In some like chamber, shadowing forth
How the daemonic rage
Imagined everything.
Benighted travellers
From markets and from fairs
Have seen his midnight candle glimmering.

Two men have founded here. A man-at-arms
Gathered a score of horse and spent his days
In this tumultuous spot,
Where through long wars and sudden night alarms
His dwindling score and he seemed castaways
Forgetting and forgot;
And I, that after me
My bodily heirs may find,
To exalt a lonely mind,
Befitting emblems of adversity.

V

The Road at My Door

An affable Irregular,
A heavily-built Falstaffian man,
Comes cracking jokes of civil war
As though to die by gunshot were
The finest play under the sun.

A brown Lieutenant and his men,
Half dressed in national uniform,
Stand at my door, and I complain
Of the foul weather, hail and rain,
A pear-tree broken by the storm.

I count those feathered balls of soot
The moor-hen guides upon the stream,
To silence the envy in my thought;
And turn towards my chamber, caught
In the cold snows of a dream.

VI

The Stare's Nest by My Window

The bees build in the crevices
Of loosening masonry, and there
The mother birds bring grubs and flies.
My wall is loosening; honey-bees,
Come build in the empty house of the stare.

We are closed in, and the key is turned
On our uncertainty; somewhere
A man is killed, or a house burned,
Yet no clear fact to be discerned:
Come build in the empty house of the stare.

A barricade of stone or of wood;
Some fourteen days of civil war;
Last night they trundled down the road
That dead young soldier in his blood:
Come build in the empty house of the stare.

We had fed the heart on fantasies,
The heart's grown brutal from the fare;
More substance in our enmities
Than in our love; O honey-bees,
Come build in the empty house of the stare.

1923

LEDA AND THE SWAN

A sudden blow: the great wings beating still
Above the staggering girl, her thighs caressed
By the dark webs, her nape caught in his bill,
He holds her helpless breast upon his breast.

How can those terrified vague fingers push
The feathered glory from her loosening thighs?
And how can body, laid in that white rush,
But feel the strange heart beating where it lies?

A shudder in the loins engenders there
The broken wall, the burning roof and tower
And Agamemnon dead.
                                    Being so caught up,
So mastered by the brute blood of the air,
Did she put on his knowledge with his power
Before the indifferent beak could let her drop?

1923

from

A MAN YOUNG AND OLD

XI

From 'Oedipus at Colonus'

Endure what life God gives and ask no longer span;
Cease to remember the delights of youth, travel-wearied
      aged man;
Delight becomes death-longing if all longing else be vain.

Even from that delight memory treasures so,
Death, despair, division of families, all entanglements
      of mankind grow,
As that old wandering beggar and these God-hated
      children know.

In the long echoing street the laughing dancers throng,
The bride is carried to the bridegroom's chamber
      through torchlight and tumultuous song;
I celebrate the silent kiss that ends short life or long.

Never to have lived is best, ancient writers say;
Never to have drawn the breath of life, never to have
      looked into the eye of day;
The second best's a gay goodnight and quickly turn away.

IN MEMORY OF EVA GORE-BOOTH AND CON MARKIEWICZ

The light of evening, Lissadell,
Great windows open to the south,
Two girls in silk kimonos, both
Beautiful, one a gazelle.
But a raving autumn shears
Blossom from the summer's wreath;
The older is condemned to death,
Pardoned, drags out lonely years
Conspiring among the ignorant.
I know not what the younger dreams —
Some vague Utopia — and she seems,
When withered old and skeleton-gaunt,
An image of such politics.
Many a time I think to seek
One or the other out and speak
Of that old Georgian mansion, mix
Pictures of the mind, recall
That table and the talk of youth,
Two girls in silk kimonos, both
Beautiful, one a gazelle.

Dear shadows, now you know it all,
All the folly of a fight
With a common wrong or right.
The innocent and the beautiful
Have no enemy but time;
Arise and bid me strike a match
And strike another till time catch;
Should the conflagration climb,
Run till all the sages know.
We the great gazebo built,
They convicted us of guilt;
Bid me strike a match and blow.

October 1927

DEATH

Nor dread nor hope attend
A dying animal;
A man awaits his end
Dreading and hoping all;
Many times he died,
Many times rose again.
A great man in his pride
Confronting murderous men
Casts derision upon
Supersession of breath;
He knows death to the bone —
Man has created death.

from

BLOOD AND THE MOON

I

Blessed be this place,
More blessed still this tower;
A bloody, arrogant power
Rose out of the race
Uttering, mastering it,
Rose like these walls from these
Storm-beaten cottages —
In mockery I have set
A powerful emblem up,
And sing it rhyme upon rhyme
In mockery of a time
Half dead at the top.

III

The purity of the unclouded moon
Has flung its arrowy shaft upon the floor.
Seven centuries have passed and it is pure,
The blood of innocence has left no stain.
There, on blood-saturated ground, have stood
Soldier, assassin, executioner,
Whether for daily pittance or in blind fear
Or out of abstract hatred, and shed blood,

But could not cast a single jet thereon.
Odour of blood on the ancestral stair!
And we that have shed none must gather there
And clamour in drunken frenzy for the moon.

SYMBOLS

A storm-beaten old watch-tower,
A blind hermit rings the hour.

All-destroying sword-blade still
Carried by the wandering fool.

Gold-sewn silk on the sword-blade,
Beauty and fool together laid.

COOLE PARK AND BALLYLEE, 1931

Under my window-ledge the waters race,
Otters below and moor-hens on the top,
Run for a mile undimmed in Heaven's face
Then darkening through 'dark' Raftery's 'cellar' drop,
Run underground, rise in a rocky place
In Coole demesne, and there to finish up
Spread to a lake and drop into a hole.
What's water but the generated soul?

Upon the border of that lake's a wood
Now all dry sticks under a wintry sun,
And in a copse of beeches there I stood,
For Nature's pulled her tragic buskin on
And all the rant's a mirror of my mood:
At sudden thunder of the mounting swan
I turned about and looked where branches break
The glittering reaches of the flooded lake.

Another emblem there! That stormy white
But seems a concentration of the sky;
And, like the soul, it sails into the sight
And in the morning's gone, no man knows why;
And is so lovely that it sets to right

What knowledge or its lack had set awry,
So arrogantly pure, a child might think
It can be murdered with a spot of ink.

Sound of a stick upon the floor, a sound
From somebody that toils from chair to chair;
Beloved books that famous hands have bound,
Old marble heads, old pictures everywhere;
Great rooms where travelled men and children found
Content or joy; a last inheritor
Where none has reigned that lacked a name and fame
Or out of folly into folly came.

A spot whereon the founders lived and died
Seemed once more dear than life; ancestral trees,
Or gardens rich in memory glorified
Marriages, alliances and families,
And every bride's ambition satisfied.
Where fashion or mere fantasy decrees
We shift about — all that great glory spent —
Like some poor Arab tribesman and his tent.

We were the last romantics — chose for theme
Traditional sanctity and loveliness;
Whatever's written in what poets name
The book of the people; whatever most can bless
The mind of man or elevate a rhyme;

But all is changed, that high horse riderless,
Though mounted in that saddle Homer rode
Where the swan drifts upon a darkening flood.

SWIFT'S EPITAPH

Swift has sailed into his rest;
Savage indignation there
Cannot lacerate his breast.
Imitate him if you dare,
World-besotted traveller; he
Served human liberty.

THE CHOICE

The intellect of man is forced to choose
Perfection of the life, or of the work,
And if it take the second must refuse
A heavenly mansion, raging in the dark.

When all that story's finished, what's the news?
In luck or out the toil has left its mark:
That old perplexity an empty purse,
Or the day's vanity, the night's remorse.

IV

My fiftieth year had come and gone,
I sat, a solitary man,
In a crowded London shop,
An open book and empty cup
On the marble table-top.

While on the shop and street I gazed
My body of a sudden blazed;
And twenty minutes more or less
It seemed, so great my happiness,
That I was blessèd and could bless.

REMORSE FOR INTEMPERATE SPEECH

I ranted to the knave and fool,
But outgrew that school,
Would transform the part,
Fit audience found, but cannot rule
My fanatic[1] heart.

I sought my betters: though in each
Fine manners, liberal speech,
Turn hatred into sport,
Nothing said or done can reach
My fanatic heart.

Out of Ireland have we come.
Great hatred, little room,
Maimed us at the start.
I carry from my mother's womb
A fanatic heart

August 28, 1931

[1] I pronounce 'fanatic' in what is, I suppose, the older and more Irish way,
so that the last line of each stanza contains but two beats.

WORDS FOR MUSIC PERHAPS

I
CRAZY JANE AND THE BISHOP

Bring me to the blasted oak
That I, midnight upon the stroke,
(*All find safety in the tomb.*)
May call down curses on his head
Because of my dear Jack that's dead.
Coxcomb was the least he said:
The solid man and the coxcomb.

Nor was he Bishop when his ban
Banished Jack the Journeyman,
(*All find safety in the tomb.*)
Nor so much as parish priest,
Yet he, an old book in his fist,
Cried that we lived like beast and beast:
The solid man and the coxcomb.

The Bishop has a skin, God knows,
Wrinkled like the foot of a goose,
(*All find safety in the tomb.*)
Nor can he hide in holy black

The heron's hunch upon his back,
But a birch-tree stood my Jack:
The solid man and the coxcomb.

Jack had my virginity,
And bids me to the oak, for he
(*All find safety in the tomb.*)
Wanders out into the night
And there is shelter under it,
But should that other come, I spit:
The solid man and the coxcomb.

V

CRAZY JANE ON GOD

That lover of a night
Came when he would,
Went in the dawning light
Whether I would or no;
Men come, men go;
All things remain in God.

Banners choke the sky;
Men-at-arms tread;
Armoured horses neigh
Where the great battle was
In the narrow pass:
All things remain in God.

Before their eyes a house
That from childhood stood
Uninhabited, ruinous,
Suddenly lit up
From door to top:
All things remain in God.

I had wild Jack for a lover;
Though like a road
That men pass over
My body makes no moan
But sings on:
All things remain in God.

VI

CRAZY JANE TALKS WITH THE BISHOP

I met the Bishop on the road
And much said he and I.
'Those breasts are flat and fallen now,
Those veins must soon be dry;
Live in a heavenly mansion,
Not in some foul sty.'

'Fair and foul are near of kin,
And fair needs foul,' I cried.
'My friends are gone, but that's a truth

Nor grave nor bed denied, .
Learned in bodily lowliness
And in the heart's pride.

'A woman can be proud and stiff
When on love intent;
But Love has pitched his mansion in
The place of excrement;
For nothing can be sole or whole
That has not been rent.'

X
HER ANXIETY

Earth in beauty dressed
Awaits returning spring.
All true love must die,
Alter at the best
Into some lesser thing.
Prove that I lie.

Such body lovers have,
Such exacting breath,
That they touch or sigh.
Every touch they give,
Love is nearer death.
Prove that I lie.

XVII
AFTER LONG SILENCE

Speech after long silence; it is right,
All other lovers being estranged or dead,
Unfriendly lamplight hid under its shade,
The curtains drawn upon unfriendly night,
That we descant and yet again descant
Upon the supreme theme of Art and Song:
Bodily decrepitude is wisdom; young
We loved each other and were ignorant.

from

A WOMAN YOUNG AND OLD

VI

CHOSEN

The lot of love is chosen. I learnt that much
Struggling for an image on the track
Of the whirling Zodiac.
Scarce did he my body touch,
Scarce sank he from the west
Or found a subterranean rest
On the maternal midnight of my breast
Before I had marked him on his northern way,
And seemed to stand although in bed I lay.

I struggled with the horror of daybreak,
I chose it for my lot! If questioned on
My utmost pleasure with a man
By some new-married bride, I take
That stillness for a theme
Where his heart my heart did seem
And both adrift on the miraculous stream
Where — wrote a learned astrologer —
The Zodiac is changed into a sphere.

A LAST CONFESSION

What lively lad most pleasured me
Of all that with me lay?
I answer that I gave my soul
And loved in misery,
But had great pleasure with a lad
That I loved bodily.

Flinging from his arms I laughed
To think his passion such
He fancied that I gave a soul
Did but our bodies touch,
And laughed upon his breast to think
Beast gave beast as much.

I gave what other women gave
That stepped out of their clothes,
But when this soul, its body off,
Naked to naked goes,
He it has found shall find therein
What none other knows,

And give his own and take his own
And rule in his own right;
And though it loved in misery

Close and cling so tight,
There's not a bird of day that dare
Extinguish that delight.

PARNELL'S FUNERAL

I

Under the Great Comedian's tomb the crowd.
A bundle of tempestuous cloud is blown
About the sky; where that is clear of cloud
Brightness remains; a brighter star shoots down;
What shudders run through all that animal blood?
What is this sacrifice? Can someone there
Recall the Cretan barb that pierced a star?

Rich foliage that the starlight glittered through,
A frenzied crowd, and where the branches sprang
A beautiful seated boy; a sacred bow;
A woman, and an arrow on a string;
A pierced boy, image of a star laid low.
That woman, the Great Mother imaging,
Cut out his heart. Some master of design
Stamped boy and tree upon Sicilian coin.

An age is the reversal of an age:
When strangers murdered Emmet, Fitzgerald, Tone,
We lived like men that watch a painted stage.
What matter for the scene, the scene once gone:
It had not touched our lives. But popular rage,

Hysterica passio dragged this quarry down.
None shared our guilt; nor did we play a part
Upon a painted stage when we devoured his heart.

Come, fix upon me that accusing eye.
I thirst for accusation. All that was sung,
All that was said in Ireland is a lie
Bred out of the contagion of the throng,
Saving the rhyme rats hear before they die.
Leave nothing but the nothings that belong
To this bare soul, let all men judge that can
Whether it be an animal or a man.

II

The rest I pass, one sentence I unsay.
Had de Valéra eaten Parnell's heart
No loose-lipped demagogue had won the day,
No civil rancour torn the land apart.

Had Cosgrave eaten Parnell's heart, the land's
Imagination had been satisfied,
Or lacking that, government in such hands,
O'Higgins its sole statesman had not died.

Had even O'Duffy — but I name no more —
Their school a crowd, his master solitude;
Through Jonathan Swift's dark grove he passed, and there
Plucked bitter wisdom that enriched his blood.

CHURCH AND STATE

Here is fresh matter, poet,
Matter for old age meet;
Might of the Church and the State,
Their mobs put under their feet.
O but heart's wine shall run pure,
Mind's bread grow sweet.

That were a cowardly song,
Wander in dreams no more;
What if the Church and the State
Are the mob that howls at the door!
Wine shall run thick to the end,
Bread taste sour.

August 1934

from
SUPERNATURAL SONGS

III

Ribh in Ecstasy

What matter that you understood no word!
Doubtless I spoke or sang what I had heard
In broken sentences. My soul had found
All happiness in its own cause or ground.
Godhead on Godhead in sexual spasm begot
Godhead. Some shadow fell. My soul forgot
Those amorous cries that out of quiet come
And must the common round of day resume.

IX

The Four Ages of Man

He with body waged a fight,
But body won; it walks upright.

Then he struggled with the heart;
Innocence and peace depart.

Then he struggled with the mind;
His proud heart he left behind.

Now his wars on God begin;
At stroke of midnight God shall win.

Meru

Civilisation is hooped together, brought
Under a rule, under the semblance of peace
By manifold illusion; but man's life is thought,
And he, despite his terror, cannot cease
Ravening through century after century,
Ravening, raging, and uprooting that he may come
Into the desolation of reality:
Egypt and Greece, good-bye, and good-bye, Rome!
Hermits upon Mount Meru or Everest,
Caverned in night under the drifted snow,
Or where that snow and winter's dreadful blast
Beat down upon their naked bodies, know
That day brings round the night, that before dawn
His glory and his monuments are gone.

LAPIS LAZULI
(*For Harry Clifton*)

I have heard that hysterical women say
They are sick of the palette and fiddle-bow,
Of poets that are always gay,
For everybody knows or else should know
That if nothing drastic is done
Aeroplane and Zeppelin will come out,
Pitch like King Billy bomb-balls in
Until the town lie beaten flat.

All perform their tragic play,
There struts Hamlet, there is Lear,
That's Ophelia, that Cordelia;
Yet they, should the last scene be there,
The great stage curtain about to drop,
If worthy their prominent part in the play,
Do not break up their lines to weep.
They know that Hamlet and Lear are gay;
Gaiety transfiguring all that dread.
All men have aimed at, found and lost;
Black out; Heaven blazing into the head:
Tragedy wrought to its uttermost.
Though Hamlet rambles and Lear rages,

And all the drop-scenes drop at once
Upon a hundred thousand stages,
It cannot grow by an inch or an ounce.

On their own feet they came, or on shipboard,
Camel-back, horse-back, ass-back, mule-back,
Old civilisations put to the sword.
Then they and their wisdom went to rack:
No handiwork of Callimachus,
Who handled marble as if it were bronze,
Made draperies that seemed to rise
When sea-wind swept the corner, stands;
His long lamp-chimney shaped like the stem
Of a slender palm, stood but a day;
All things fall and are built again,
And those that build them again are gay.

Two Chinamen, behind them a third,
Are carved in lapis lazuli,
Over them flies a long-legged bird,
A symbol of longevity;
The third, doubtless a serving-man,
Carries a musical instrument.

Every discoloration of the stone,
Every accidental crack or dent,
Seems a water-course or an avalanche,

Or lofty slope where it still snows
Though doubtless plum or cherry-branch
Sweetens the little half-way house
Those Chinamen climb towards, and I
Delight to imagine them seated there;
There, on the mountain and the sky,
On all the tragic scene they stare.
One asks for mournful melodies;
Accomplished fingers begin to play.
Their eyes mid many wrinkles, their eyes,
Their ancient, glittering eyes, are gay.

SWEET DANCER

The girl goes dancing there
On the leaf-sown, new-mown, smooth
Grass plot of the garden;
Escaped from bitter youth,
Escaped out of her crowd,
Or out of her black cloud.
Ah, dancer, ah, sweet dancer!

If strange men come from the house
To lead her away, do not say
That she is happy being crazy;
Lead them gently astray;
Let her finish her dance,
Let her finish her dance.
Ah, dancer, ah, sweet dancer!

THE GREAT DAY

Hurrah for revolution and more cannon-shot!
A beggar upon horseback lashes a beggar on foot.
Hurrah for revolution and cannon come again!
The beggars have changed places, but the lash goes on.

THE OLD STONE CROSS

A statesman is an easy man,
He tells his lies by rote;
A journalist makes up his lies
And takes you by the throat;
So stay at home and drink your beer
And let the neighbours vote,
> *Said the man in the golden breastplate*
> *Under the old stone Cross.*

Because this age and the next age
Engender in the ditch,
No man can know a happy man
From any passing wretch;
If Folly link with Elegance
No man knows which is which,
> *Said the man in the golden breastplate*
> *Under the old stone Cross.*

But actors lacking music
Do most excite my spleen,
They say it is more human
To shuffle, grunt and groan,
Not knowing what unearthly stuff

Rounds a mighty scene,
>   *Said the man in the golden breastplate*
>   *Under the old stone Cross.*

ARE YOU CONTENT?

I call on those that call me son,
Grandson, or great-grandson,
On uncles, aunts, great-uncles or great-aunts,
To judge what I have done.
Have I, that put it into words,
Spoilt what old loins have sent?
Eyes spiritualised by death can judge,
I cannot, but I am not content.

He that in Sligo at Drumcliff
Set up the old stone Cross,
That red-headed rector in County Down,
A good man on a horse,
Sandymount Corbets, that notable man
Old William Pollexfen,
The smuggler Middleton, Butlers far back,
Half legendary men.

Infirm and aged I might stay
In some good company,
I who have always hated work,
Smiling at the sea,
Or demonstrate in my own life

What Robert Browning meant
By an old hunter talking with Gods;
But I am not content.

THE STATUES

Pythagoras planned it. Why did the people stare?
His numbers, though they moved or seemed to move
In marble or in bronze, lacked character.
But boys and girls, pale from the imagined love
Of solitary beds, knew what they were,
That passion could bring character enough,
And pressed at midnight in some public place
Live lips upon a plummet-measured face.

No! Greater than Pythagoras, for the men
That with a mallet or a chisel modelled these
Calculations that look but casual flesh, put down
All Asiatic vague immensities,
And not the banks of oars that swam upon
The many-headed foam at Salamis.
Europe put off that foam when Phidias
Gave women dreams and dreams their looking-glass.

One image crossed the many-headed, sat
Under the tropic shade, grew round and slow,
No Hamlet thin from eating flies, a fat
Dreamer of the Middle Ages. Empty eyeballs knew
That knowledge increases unreality, that

Mirror on mirror mirrored is all the show.
When gong and conch declare the hour to bless
Grimalkin crawls to Buddha's emptiness.

When Pearse summoned Cuchulain to his side,
What stalked through the Post Office? What intellect,
What calculation, number, measurement, replied?
We Irish, born into that ancient sect
But thrown upon this filthy modern tide
And by its formless spawning fury wrecked,
Climb to our proper dark, that we may trace
The lineaments of a plummet-measured face.

April 9, 1938

WHY SHOULD NOT OLD MEN BE MAD?

Why should not old men be mad?
Some have known a likely lad
That had a sound fly-fisher's wrist
Turn to a drunken journalist;
A girl that knew all Dante once
Live to bear children to a dunce;
A Helen of social welfare dream,
Climb on a wagonette to scream.
Some think it a matter of course that chance
Should starve good men and bad advance,
That if their neighbours figured plain,
As though upon a lighted screen,
No single story would they find
Of an unbroken happy mind,
A finish worthy of the start.
Young men know nothing of this sort,
Observant old men know it well;
And when they know what old books tell,
And that no better can be had,
Know why an old man should be mad.

POLITICS

'In our time the destiny of man presents its meaning in political terms.' — Thomas Mann

How can I, that girl standing there,
My attention fix
On Roman or on Russian
Or on Spanish politics?
Yet here's a travelled man that knows
What he talks about,
And there's a politician
That has read and thought,
And maybe what they say is true
Of war and war's alarms,
But O that I were young again
And held her in my arms!

CUCHULAIN COMFORTED

A man that had six mortal wounds, a man
Violent and famous, strode among the dead;
Eyes stared out of the branches and were gone.

Then certain Shrouds that muttered head to head
Came and were gone. He leant upon a tree
As though to meditate on wounds and blood.

A Shroud that seemed to have authority
Among those bird-like things came, and let fall
A bundle of linen. Shrouds by two and three

Came creeping up because the man was still.
And thereupon that linen-carrier said:
'Your life can grow much sweeter if you will

'Obey our ancient rule and make a shroud;
Mainly because of what we only know
The rattle of those arms makes us afraid.

'We thread the needles' eyes, and all we do
All must together do.' That done, the man
Took up the nearest and began to sew.

'Now must we sing and sing the best we can,
But first you must be told our character:
Convicted cowards all, by kindred slain

'Or driven from home and left to die in fear.'
They sang, but had nor human tunes nor words,
Though all was done in common as before;

They had changed their throats and had the throats of
       birds.

    January 13, 1939

from
UNDER BEN BULBEN

VI

Under bare Ben Bulben's head
In Drumcliff churchyard Yeats is laid.
An ancestor was rector there
Long years ago, a church stands near,
By the road an ancient cross.
No marble, no conventional phrase;
On limestone quarried near the spot
By his command these words are cut:

> *Cast a cold eye*
> *On life, on death.*
> *Horseman, pass by!*

September 4, 1938

Bibliographical Note

There are many editions of the *Collected Poems,* now available in paperback, including *W.B.Yeats: Collected Poems,* edited by Augustine Martin (Arena) and *W.B.Yeats: The Poems. A New Edition* (Macmillan), edited by Richard J Finneran. The most widely used edition remains the *Collected Poems* (Macmillan), edited by Thomas Mark and the poet's widow, Mrs Georgie Yeats, in 1950.

The most approachable of Yeats scholars is Richard Ellmann and his two books, *Yeats: The Man and the Masks* and *The Identity of Yeats* are strongly recommended, along with the writings of A.N.Jeffares. Augustine Martin's introductory study of Yeats is useful. Roy Foster, the historian, is writing the authorised biography, and Terence Brown, the literary critic and cultural historian, is also at work on a biographical study of Yeats. His *Ireland: A Social and Cultural History 1922-1985* is essential background reading.

Some of the sharpest criticism of Yeats can be found in the work of Seamus Deane (*Celtic Revivals* and *A Short History of Irish Literature*).

Other critics whose work should be consulted are Edna Longley (*Poetry in the Wars*), Tom Paulin (*Minotaur*), Edward W. Said (*Yeats and Decolonization*), and F.S.L. Lyons (*Culture and Anarchy in Ireland 1890-1939*). W.J. McCormack's *The Battle of the Books* summarises, amongst many other issues, the dispute over Yeats's legacy while *The Field Day Anthology of Irish Writing* contains a valuable reading of Yeats's poetry by Seamus Heaney, always a reliable guide to poetry of the first order.